C000003591

Heaven

Gwynn Williams

**Translated by
Kitty Lloyd Jones**

BRYNTIRION PRESS

© Gwynn Williams 2000
First published, 2000
ISBN 1 85049 169 0

Cover photograph: Paul Shepherd
Cover design: Phil Boorman @ burgum boorman ltd

Bible quotations are taken from
the Revised Authorised Version

Published by the Bryntirion Press
Bryntirion, Bridgend CF31 4DX, Wales, UK
Printed by Creative Print & Design (Wales) Limited

Contents

Preface

In August 1992 it was my privilege to give a series of addresses in the Welsh Conference of the Evangelical Movement of Wales on the theme of heaven. These addresses were subsequently published in Welsh in 1994.

I am greatly indebted to Kitty Lloyd Jones for taking on the onerous task of translating that book into English.

I also wish to thank all the staff at Bryntirion Press who have been involved in the production of this volume.

I trust that the book will be an encouragement to all of us as we pilgrim through this present life.

Gwynn Williams
June 2000

1
Heaven:
who will be there?

What, I wonder, is your spiritual condition? Perhaps you are on top of the world: your heart is warm and full of the joy of the gospel, and you are bursting with energy, enthusiasm and unflagging zeal to further the work of God's kingdom. Or maybe you are in the doldrums: although you sincerely wish things were different, you are cold and apathetic, your heart is hard and your spirit low, and so far as the work of the kingdom is concerned you lack the motivation and the energy to do anything of consequence. Indeed, so low and dejected do you feel that sometimes you are driven to doubt the very basics of your faith.

Between those two extremes there is a wide range of varying conditions. I would hazard a guess that most of us are nearer to the frigid than the torrid zone; much more likely to be low in spirit than euphoric; lacking in energy, zeal and enthusiasm rather than bursting with tireless activity.

There are many factors that affect our spiritual condition. For instance, one thing that doubtless has affected many of us is the kind of year we have been through. For some, perhaps, it has been a very difficult year. Stress and strain at work, or possibly over-work, has had a harmful effect on both our health and our constitution. Perhaps there have been family worries—worries about health, worries about children or parents. Or has there been a bereavement—a dear one taken suddenly, or perhaps after prolonged suffering? Or could it be some failure or disappointment

—something we had set our heart on doing or achieving came to nothing? All these various difficult providences can affect our spiritual condition, sap our energy and make us feel low in spirit.

Another factor that affects us is the spiritual condition of our country. Looking at present-day Wales we would have to be completely insensitive not to be saddened by its sorry plight. It is a sad day for our nation: its moral standards are constantly falling; lawlessness and violence are ever increasing.

Even when we look at the religious world we find no consolation. The pundits tell us that Welsh nonconformity is slowly grinding to a halt. We were all aware that there had been something radically wrong with that nonconformity for a century; yet we cannot but feel troubled that such a great phenomenon, which influenced our country for good over many centuries, has practically disappeared from our land. It saddens one to think that the evangelical Christian religion, which in the past was such a mighty force, is running out of steam. Contemplating its demise cannot but contribute to our state of spiritual depression, to the way we feel in our day and age.

Then, of course, there is that other contributory factor, namely, the sorry state of the churches to which we belong. We have to be absolutely honest with one another and confess that they leave a lot to be desired. We as preachers are not setting Wales on fire; it would be presumption on our part to think that we were even on the verge of doing so. Our preaching is correct enough; sometimes it can be quite interesting; but very rarely is there that vital spark. And what about the prayer meeting? Occasionally we feel that there is a blessing, but if we are honest would we not confess that we sometimes feel bored in the prayer meeting? We know how we feel inwardly; there is a depression and a longing for better things.

You will agree with me, I'm sure, that there are two things that we as evangelical Christians need at the present time. In the first place, we need something that will lift our hearts and restore the joy of our salvation, putting a spring in our footsteps once more, rekindling the fire in our heart and putting a new song on our lips. But we also need something that will encourage us to work tirelessly in our land during the coming years, despite the opposition that will doubtless increase as time passes. We need encouragement, do we not, to work diligently in difficult days and in the face of opposition.

An irrelevant subject?

What I should like us to do is to meditate a little on heaven. I feel certain that many people would consider such a thing a futile exercise. They would rather make a list of the world's problems, arguing that it would be much more profitable to tackle some of them. But I hope, if the Lord sees fit to bless us, that by the end of our meditation we shall realise that to think a little about heaven will enable us to deal with present-day problems more effectively than by endlessly talking about them.

First of all, I would like to ask some pertinent questions. When did you last think of heaven? When did you last hear a sermon on the subject? Doubtless you have all heard a preacher make passing reference to heaven; indeed it would be well-nigh impossible for any preacher not to mention the place in the course of a sermon. Perhaps you sometimes think fleetingly about heaven as you read your Bible and pray. But I have the feeling that when we contemplate heaven a certain shyness comes over us; we have become too bashful to think or talk much about it—and we preachers are as guilty of this as the members of our congregations.

I believe that the reasons for this bashfulness arise from the world we live in. In the first place, I believe, we have succumbed to the oppressive mindset of a secular, materialistic age, a mindset for which nothing exists other than this present world of time and space. There is no eternity, no supernatural, and therefore no heaven. Those who think in this way are only too ready to make fun of simple-minded people like us who continue to believe that such things exist; and as a result we feel oppressed. We live amongst people who believe that after death there is *nothing*.

In this kind of situation we can feel pressurised as Christians, and that pressure may cause us to have doubts. We begin to wonder whether the secular, modern man is right after all. Then, of course, once doubts creep in, we feel guilty, and there is the tendency to push the whole question of heaven into the background and to begin thinking about the 'safer' themes of the Christian gospel, especially our responsibilities in *this* world. Added to this is the anxiety not to be considered odd. Granted, people consider us odd because we claim to be evangelical Christians; but going out of our way to be odd is a totally different matter. And people who talk about heaven in this day and age are a little bit odd, are they not?

Not only are we oppressed by the secular mind, but there is oppression of a different kind coming from another direction, namely, that of the traditional religious person. How often have we been accused of being 'too heavenly-minded to be of any earthly use', not by the secularists but by religious people? We must confess that the saying does have some truth in it; there is a certain kind of pietistic Christian who is of little use to anyone. But the saying cuts closer to the bone than that. Some years ago there was an all-out attack on what was called 'succour religion'. The evangelical faith was ridiculed as a kind of succour or prop for people in the midst of life's problems, a means of escape. Quoting Marx, they dubbed the evangelical religion 'the opium of the people', a sort of drug that makes us insensitive to life's problems, allowing us to get on with our small, private, religious life without any radical concern to address social injustices—with no desire to deal with famine, poverty and the world's problems.

This accusation oppressed us to such an extent that we were driven to say, 'That is not our religion. We have a robust religion which deals with today's problems', and we proceeded to prove this. And the consequence? Heaven was quietly pushed into the background, depriving us of one vital element of the remedy which encourages the Christian to labour while he is still on this earth.

Our intention, therefore, in this series of addresses is to try to meet this need, and to do so without apology either to the secular person or to the traditional religious person. We quote the words of C. S. Lewis in his book *Mere Christianity*:

> If you read history, you will find that the Christians who did most for the present world were those who thought most of the next. The apostles themselves, who set on foot the conversion of the Roman Empire, the great men who made the Middle Ages, the English evangelicals who abolished the slave trade, all left their mark on the earth precisely because their minds were occupied with heaven.

The same author wrote these pointed words: 'It is since Christians have largely ceased to think of the other world that they have become so ineffective in this.' Our intention, therefore, is to turn our sights heavenward, hoping at the same time to keep our feet solidly on the ground.

When we turn to the New Testament, we find heaven mentioned time after time. The parables of the Lord Jesus Christ, for instance, are mostly parables about heaven; the epistles are full of references to the glory to come; and when we come to the book of Revelation we see little else but heaven. Turning to our Welsh hymns, we find it difficult to find a single example of a hymn that does not contain in one of its verses the word 'heaven' or 'heavens' or 'heavenly'—and it doesn't have to be a hymn about

11

death and eternity. Welsh hymnody is saturated with heaven; our attention is drawn to it time and time again.

Heaven—a definition

The first thing we must do is to define what exactly we mean by heaven. As we all know, the word 'heaven' is sometimes used for the firmament or the sky. Obviously we shall not be dealing with that—the sun moving across the heaven or the rains descending from heaven. In this series of addresses we shall use the word 'heaven' to describe the final state of Christian believers. Thomas Charles in his Biblical Dictionary (*Geiriadur Ysgrythurol*) defines heaven as 'the place prepared by God since the foundation of the world to be an eternal dwelling place for the chosen angels and all those that are saved, in blessedness and in the presence of God'.

According to Thomas Charles, heaven is where God has his dwelling and where his people will one day dwell with him. As we know, there are other words used in Scripture. Jesus Christ, when speaking to the thief on the cross, uses the word 'paradise', that is, the eternal and glorious dwelling place of the saints. What kind of place will it be? The Greeks, who had some notion of heaven, thought of it as a spiritual place where the souls of men would dwell. They, of course, despised the body and could not contemplate the idea of bodies in heaven; their heaven, therefore, was a place for souls only. But when we come to the Word of God we are presented with a totally different picture of the final state. Indeed, it is to be found even in the Old Testament: 'For behold, I create new heavens and a new earth; and the former shall not be remembered or come to mind' (Isaiah 65:17). Throughout the Scriptures—the Hebrew background, the Jewish and Christian eras—we see the concept of re-creating, the concept of a new earth. When we come to the second epistle of Peter we find that a reference to the destruction of this world by heat is followed by these words: 'Nevertheless we . . . look for new heavens and a new earth in which righteousness dwells' (2 Peter 3:13). In Revelation 21:1 we are again reminded of the coming 'new heaven' and 'new earth'.

Associated with all this is the resurrection of the dead. The souls of believers, which have departed their earthly bodies in death, will be reunited with their resurrected bodies, and those resurrected bodies will dwell in the new world for ever and ever. Heaven is none other than that 'new earth'—the final and everlasting state of the saints.

But what happens to the believer between death and the resurrection of the body? Some have argued that when a person dies the soul goes into a state of unconscious sleep ('soul-sleep'), consequently losing its sense of time, and the next thing it is conscious of is its resurrected body. Thus, for the person who has died it is as though, to all intents and purposes, both death and resurrection occur simultaneously, but in the realm of time there has been soul-sleep. Others, as we know, disagree, pointing out that Scripture speaks of the soul being awake and conscious in its state of existence between death and the resurrection of the body. Scripture does not tell us much about this, but Jesus Christ said to the thief on the cross, 'Today you will be with me in paradise', which implies that he would experience something that very day. Paul says 'to die is gain' because being with Christ is 'much better'. We have reason to believe, therefore, that there is a state for souls between death and the resurrection that enables them to enjoy some kind of paradise, although Scripture does not fully explain its nature. Then comes the resurrection of the body and the new earth, the final everlasting state.

We shall use the word 'heaven' not for that brief period of time, whether unconscious or otherwise, between death and the resurrection, but for that final state at the end of time, when the whole history of this world will have come to a close, when God's new creation will have come into existence, and the saints will be in the presence of God and of the Lamb.

Who will be there?

Before we turn our attention to what heaven is like, there is another fundamental and all-important question that has to be faced. How many of us will find consolation in all this? Who will be in heaven? The only people that will take comfort as they think of heaven will be those who are certain they are going there! If you are not convinced that you are going there, then you will find this topic exceedingly boring, even distressing. Nothing could be worse or more frustrating than catching a glimpse of this glorious place and yet being uncertain whether you will be there.

So the first question is, Who will be there? It has been popular among Welsh religious people to believe that everyone goes to heaven, that everybody will eventually arrive there. This is the kind of reasoning. God is the Father of all, and therefore we are all God's children; God is love, and it is inconceivable that a loving God should cast anyone out of his presence for eternity. And so, according to this view, everybody will end up in heaven, and we can all take comfort.

To confront this argument, we have to consider a number of Christian doctrines. In the first place, Scripture tells us perfectly clearly that we are not all God's children. Paul, writing to the Ephesians, says that we were once the 'children of wrath'. Notice that he says 'we'. Paul is not only referring to the pagan Ephesians but is including himself. Who was Paul? He had been a religious Pharisee. Yet what he says, in effect, is this: not only were you Ephesians the children of wrath, but the same was true of me, the religious Pharisee. And Jesus, speaking to the Pharisees on one occasion, tells them bluntly that they are 'of their father Satan'. Quite clearly, then, neither Jesus Christ nor Paul believed that all without exception were God's children. At the beginning

14

of his Gospel, John says this: 'as many as received him, to them he gave the right to become children of God'. That is, if you want to be God's children something has to happen to you; you have to be *given* something before you can enter the family. Scripture is absolutely clear on this matter.

In the second place, we must point out that Scripture speaks of another place side by side with heaven. Nearly every time Scripture refers to heaven—and this is especially true of the parables—it also refers to hell. And the idea that we get from reading about hell in Scripture is that it is not an empty place. If the concept that everyone goes to heaven were true, then hell would be empty; but that is not what we read. And so the question arises, Who is going to heaven?

Another popular view, as we know, is that the people found in heaven will be those who have *worked* their way there. You know the picture. We have all, as it were, been born on a level plain; before us is the mountain of life, and at its summit is heaven. Our task is to climb that mountain, and if during our lifetime we have climbed well enough, we shall reach the entrance gates to everlasting rest. It does not matter what religion we follow; so long as it enables us to wend our way up the mountain any religion will do. After all, there are many paths leading to the top of Snowdon. The all-important thing is to be sincere, to be in earnest. And, of course, that means putting one's religion into practice by showing kindness and doing good—climbing the mountain in the hope that one day we shall reach the summit.

Has there ever been a religion more hopeless than that? Imagine a person who takes that standpoint. If God in his mercy were to allow him to have a glimpse of heaven, and if he were to become excited by what he had seen, then he would say, 'I've had a glimpse of heaven, but I don't know whether I'll get there. I'm not certain that I've done enough.' Poor man, thinking of heaven would be more likely to lower his spirits than raise them!

But, as we know, that is not what we find in Scripture. Heaven is not something a man earns but something he receives. You remember the words in Romans 6:23—'For the wages of sin is death, but the gift of God is eternal life in Christ Jesus our Lord.' That life begins here on earth, but it comes in its fulness in heaven. 'For by grace you have been saved through faith, and that not of yourselves; it is the gift of God, not of works, lest anyone should boast' (Ephesians 2:8-9). You remember also the parable in Matthew 20. The man hires labourers: some come early in the morning and go to work in the vineyard, some come about the third hour, some about the sixth, some about the ninth, and some even at the eleventh hour. At the end of the day the time comes to pay the expectant labourers for their work. According to the parable each receives a penny. What they received bore no relationship to the work that had been done. Rather it reflected the heart of the owner, who wished to give them all a full day's wage. That is heaven. It doesn't matter when the gift is given to you; at the end of the day it comes in its fullness to each one who receives it. It is a gift, not something a person earns.

How does one come to possess the gift? How can I be certain that there will be a heaven for me? Listen to the words of Jesus Christ: 'In my Father's house are many mansions; if it were not so, I would have told you. I go to prepare a place for you. And if I go and prepare a place for you, I will come again and receive you to myself; that where I am, there you may be also. And where I go you know, and the way you know' (John 14:2-4). But it is not quite so simple as that. 'Thomas said to him, "Lord, we do not know where you are going, and how can we know the way?"' The answer is this: 'I am the way, the truth, and the life. No man comes to the Father, except through me.' What is heaven? It is the dwelling place of God, and therefore by coming to the Father we are going to heaven. But we must go by the prescribed road. 'I am the way,' says Jesus Christ.

Thou art the Way, to Thee alone
From sin and death we flee;
And he who would the Father seek
Must seek Him, Lord, by Thee.

G. W. Doane

If you are on this way you can be certain of heaven.

How do we get on this road? According to John, 'as many as received him, to them he gave the right to become children of God'. The question that each one of us must ask before we can begin to think about heaven is, Have we received Jesus Christ? 'For God so loved the world that he gave his only begotten Son, that whoever believes in him should not perish but have everlasting life' (John 3:16). Have we come to the point of believing in Christ for our eternal life and salvation, for the forgiveness of our sins? If we can say 'I believe'—and heaven is for those who can— then it is as certain as anything can be. It is Christ himself who said, 'I go to prepare a place for you.' Who are you going to believe, the secularists or Christ? Who is going to influence you, the religious people who say 'too heavenly-minded to be of any earthly use', or Christ, who told his disciples, 'I go to prepare a place for you . . . that where I am, there you may be also'? And he said this in order to comfort and encourage them as they faced the prospect of his death.

May I read a quotation from John Bunyan's *Pilgrim's Progress*? Towards the end of the book we read that Christian and his friend have reached heaven. This is how John Bunyan describes their triumphant entry:

I saw in my dream, that these two men went in at the Gate; and lo! as they entered they were transfigured, and they had raiment put on that shone like gold. There were also that met them with harps and crowns, and gave them to them, the harps to praise

17

withal, and the crowns in token of honour. Then I heard in my dream, that all the bells in the City rang again for joy; and that it was said unto them, '*Enter ye into the joy of the Lord.*' I also heard the men themselves, that they sang with a loud voice, saying, '*Blessing, honour, glory, and power, be unto him that sitteth upon the throne, and to the Lamb, for ever and ever.*'

Now, just as the Gates opened to let in the men, I looked in after them; and, behold, the City shone like the sun; the streets also were paved with gold, and in them walked many men with crowns on their heads, palms in their hands, and golden harps to sing praises withal.

There were also of them that had wings, and they answered one another without intermission, saying, '*Holy, holy, holy, is the Lord.*' And after that, they shut up the Gates: which when I had seen, I wished myself among them.

Unbeliever—you who as yet have found believing difficult—it is worth your continuing to listen in case your eyes should be opened. All I shall do is remind you of what Scripture says, and it is possible that God will open the door slightly and give you that glimpse of heaven which will make you wish, with Bunyan, that you were among the redeemed, and kindle within you a determination not to rest until you have found salvation.

You might ask, Will there be room for me there? Friend, heaven is an enormous place: 'in my Father's house are many mansions', said Jesus Christ. God told Abraham how numerous his children would be (that is, his children by faith, the elect that would be in heaven): they would be as numerous as the sand of the sea or the stars of the firmament. And John in his Revelation saw a multitude that no one could count. It is a big place; do not entertain the thought that heaven is small. God's grace is never-ending, and men and women are invited to believe in Christ and are welcomed there.

Those of you who are believers, all I can do is remind you of what you already know. I believe that we need to look to God, trusting that he will open the gates a little so that we may be lifted up and, as a result, go home with a new zeal to labour and strive in present-day Wales. The day is far gone in this land of ours, and we need strong, valiant, diligent saints to face the onerous task ahead. May God in his mercy speak to us.

2
The things that shall be no more

As I have already mentioned, our task will be to meditate on heaven. Now, as you are all aware, Scripture is full of references to meditating and meditation, but do we as Christians know what it is to meditate? Unless we do, how can we hope to accomplish our proposed task? Looking back over the history of the church, I have no doubt that much of the enthusiasm and diligence of the past derived from the fact that the saints spent time in meditation. They meditated on all aspects of the Christian faith, but in some cases specifically on heaven.

In 1991 we were celebrating the tercentenary of the death of Richard Baxter, a Puritan who ministered in Kidderminster during the seventeenth century. Now Kidderminster was a sizeable town of some two thousand adults (not to mention the numerous children families had at that time), and during the fourteen-year period of his ministry over half of those people experienced conversion. Obviously Baxter was a tireless preacher and minister. After that fruitful period, thrown out of his pastorate by the church authorities, he spent the remainder of his life studying divinity. It so happens that he was the most prolific of the divines who wrote in the English language; the amount of work produced by this one man was phenomenal.

But what makes Baxter's enormous amount of work the more astounding is what we know of the state of his health. This is what we are told: 'He was a chronically sick Puritan, tubercular from his teens and suffering from dyspepsia, kidney stones, headaches, toothaches, sore limbs, intermittent bleeding at his extremities and other troubles—and all before the days of pain-killing drugs.' We cannot but feel sorry for the man; he must have been in constant pain. And yet there was all that industry, both during his fourteen years as a minister and subsequently when he was ceaselessly writing books on theology. We wonder how he was able to think, let alone concentrate, under such difficult circumstances. What was his secret? It was this: Richard Baxter spent half an hour every day meditating on heaven, and that half-hour of meditation in the midst of all his suffering was sufficient encouragement to him to do a good day's work for the furthering of the kingdom of Jesus Christ.

How did Baxter reach the conclusion that a period of meditation would better enable him to accomplish his onerous tasks? It was a verse in the book of Genesis that spoke to him—'And Isaac went out to meditate in the field in the evening' (Genesis 24:63) —and he was challenged to emulate the patriarch. He decided to meditate on heaven, and in *The Saints' Everlasting Rest*, one of the classics of the English language which he wrote later in life, he shares with us the fruits of his meditations. We thus have evidence that meditating on heaven has produced at least one veritable giant of a minister and divine. And it may surprise some of you to learn that in the middle of his *Institutes*—books which we tend to think of as tomes of ponderous theology—Calvin also has a chapter on 'Meditation on a Future Life'.

Now we know that in Scripture the words 'meditate', 'meditating' and 'meditation' occur over and over again. You remember how young Joshua, when the responsibility of leading the nation had fallen on his shoulders after the death of Moses, was urged to meditate. 'This Book of the Law shall not depart from your mouth, but you shall meditate in it day and night, that you may observe to do according to all that is written in it. For then you

21

will make your way prosperous, and then you will have good success.' You need to meditate, says God, and if you do so you will succeed—your meditations will bear fruit. The just man, according to the first Psalm, meditates continually—'But his delight is in the law of the Lord, and in his law he meditates day and night'—the result being that he prospers in whatever he does.

But what does meditating mean? Well, it means more than just reading—reading a book or reading the Scriptures. It means more than understanding what we read. It means more than remembering what has been read or heard. What exactly is it then? To answer the question we can do no better than turn once more to Thomas Charles: 'Meditating on spiritual things can be likened to the work of the stomach digesting its food and adapting it to become sustenance for the body and nutrition for the mind.' 'Eating', says Charles, 'will avail us nothing without the stomach's digestion. Likewise, listening and reading, without frequent and serious meditation, are likely to be both fruitless and useless to the soul.'

I have often wondered why all the sermons we have heard and all the books we have read have not had a greater effect on us. I have come to the same conclusion as Thomas Charles: that we have heard too many sermons and read too many books without meditating sufficiently on what we have heard and read. We have not succeeded in digesting and assimilating what we have 'eaten', and consequently it has been of little benefit. There will be little growth or fruit unless meditating becomes an integral part of our spiritual life.

What then is meditating? To put it simply, it is talking to oneself about spiritual things. In Psalm 77 we find this verse: 'I call to remembrance my song in the night; I meditate within my heart, and my spirit makes diligent search' (v.6). Again in verse 12 we read: 'I will also meditate on all your work, and talk of your deeds.' The Psalmist is soliloquising; he is having a discourse with himself about the things of the soul and the things of God. How many of you fancy yourselves as preachers? Well, here's your chance! Talk to yourselves and preach to yourselves! That is what meditating is.

The Psalmist, of course, does this over and over again. 'Why are you cast down, O my soul? And why are you disquieted within me? Hope in God; for I shall yet praise him, the help of my countenance and my God' (Psalm 42:11). He is meditating and addressing his soul. In Psalm 103 we find, 'Bless the LORD, O my soul'. The Psalmist is not singing praises to God, neither is he encouraging his congregation, but he is talking to himself. 'Bless the LORD, O my soul; and all that is within me, bless his holy name! Bless the LORD, O my soul, and forget not all his benefits.' And he goes on talking to himself: 'Who forgives all your iniquities, who heals all your diseases', and so on.

Meditating on heaven, therefore, is talking to ourselves about heaven. Let us follow Baxter's example and set aside half an hour each day to meditate on that blessed place that has been prepared for the saints. And when Baxter talked to himself about the place, not only did he lose sight of his problems, but an inexplicable energy was released, so that he came out of his closet 'as a strong man to run a race'.

Five things that we shall not find in heaven

Let us begin by meditating for a short time on what will *not* be in heaven. We have already seen that our spiritual condition, our lowness of spirit, our tiredness, our lack of enthusiasm, may often be caused by environmental conditions—factors within our lives and around us that oppress and tyrannise the soul. Now we need to look more closely at some of these.

1) Difficult providences

In the third chapter of the book of Genesis, verses 17-19, we find these words spoken by God to Adam after he had fallen into sin:

Because you have heeded the voice of your wife, and have eaten from the tree of which I commanded you, saying, 'You shall not eat from it': Cursed is the ground for your sake; in toil you shall eat from it all the days of your life. Both thorns also and thistles it shall bring forth for you, and you shall eat the herb of the field. In the sweat of your face you shall eat bread till you return to the ground, for out of it you were taken; for dust you are, and to dust you shall return.

One of the consequences of the fall was that the whole of creation came under a curse: that is, creation no longer co-operated with man. The created world, as it were, is set against mankind. There are difficult providences; these are common to all and befall us all. Such providences come not according to or contrary to our deserts, but in the order of things. All manner of things are signs of this curse. For instance, some of us come into the world with the effect of the curse already apparent: born with a disability, physical or mental, we have to contend with suffering and difficulties for the rest of our days. Then, of course, there is sickness and disease; these too are part and parcel of the curse on creation. Accidents happen, tragedies and disappointments, and there are failures. All these things come as a result of the curse that followed man's disobedience and his falling into sin.

Such are the difficult providences that we all have to contend with whilst in this world. Now we know what happens when difficult things come our way. More often than not the first question asked is, Why me? That is man's natural reaction, to question the difficult providence. But one difficult providence is frequently accompanied or followed by others; they come in droves, and we feel ourselves downtrodden and oppressed. There is agony of soul; there is listlessness; there is a sapping of spiritual energy—and all this has a harmful effect on our Christian life and service.

24

What remedy is there for difficult providences? Have you tried meditating on heaven? Consider these words from the book of Revelation:

> And he showed me a pure river of the water of life, clear as crystal, proceeding from the throne of God and of the Lamb. In the middle of its street, and on either side of the river, was the tree of life, which bore twelve fruits, each tree yielding its fruit every month. And the leaves of the tree were for the healing of the nations. And there shall be no more curse (Revelation 22:1-3).

The curse and the difficult providences referred to in Genesis will continue until that glorious day when there will be a new earth and a new heaven for the people of God. 'And there shall be no more curse': no disability, no sickness, no accidents, no disappointments. All will have gone away; the curse will have gone! The wonderful prophetic words of Isaiah will come to pass:

> The wolf also shall dwell with the lamb, the leopard shall lie down with the young goat, the calf and the young lion and the fatling together; and a little child shall lead them. The cow and the bear shall graze; their young ones shall lie down together; and the lion shall eat straw like the ox. The nursing child shall play by the cobra's hole, and the weaned child shall put his hand in the viper's den. They shall not hurt nor destroy in all my holy mountain, for the earth shall be full of the knowledge of the LORD as the waters cover the sea (Isaiah 11:6-9).

Should there come a day in your life when difficult providences are overbearing, take a moment to meditate on heaven, and you will come out of your room with a new resolve to persevere right to the end, knowing that there is a day coming when you will no longer have to bear the curse.

And we from the wilds of the desert
Shall flee to the land of the blest;
Life's tears shall be changed to rejoicing,
Its labours and toil into rest.
There we shall find refuge eternal
From sin, from affliction, from pain,
And in the sweet love of the Saviour
A joy without end shall attain.

David Charles, tr. by Lewis Edwards

2) The presence of sin

Do you feel as depressed as I do after watching a television news programme for half an hour? All you see is fighting; all you hear about are the 'affairs' of world leaders, the latest murder in Britain, the latest baby to be snatched, the latest bomb to explode. The news is but a catalogue of sin and its consequences, the horror and evil of sin. Seeing this, how can one but feel depressed?— it casts a dark cloud over everything.

Perhaps there are some of you who, day in and day out, are having to put up with uncouth colleagues in the workplace. Smutty jokes and suggestive talk are enough to lower the spirit of the strongest saint. True, we have a tendency to become hardened to these things; but there is a certain sensitivity, and the presence of evil in society wearies and troubles our souls.

In the second chapter of his second epistle (one of the darkest chapters in the whole of Scripture), Peter speaks of Lot. He was, admittedly, not the greatest of the world's saints (we gather from the Genesis narrative that he was much conditioned by the standards of his day), yet he merits the apostle's admiration. Says Peter (2 Peter 2:7-8) 'and [God] delivered righteous Lot, who was oppressed by the filthy conduct of the wicked (for that righteous man, dwelling among them, tormented his righteous soul from day to day by seeing and hearing their lawless deeds).' Although Lot's standards were pretty low, he was still sensitive and could feel vexed in his soul by the sight and sound of their lawless deeds. Do we sometimes feel like Lot? Nothing is more likely to make us low-spirited than having to live in such circumstances all the time.

What is the remedy? Have you ever tried meditating on heaven? This is what we read in the book of Revelation: 'Its gates shall not be shut at all by day (there shall be no night there). And they shall bring the glory and the honour of the nations into it. But there shall by no means enter it anything that defiles, or causes an abomination or a lie, but only those who are written in the Lamb's book of life' (21:25-27). And later we read: 'But outside are dogs and sorcerers and sexually immoral and murderers and idolaters, and whoever loves and practises a lie' (22:15). We shall not have to suffer for ever, nor shall our souls always be troubled. There is a heaven, and in heaven all those things that trouble us will be debarred, for heaven is a place of holiness and perfection. So when at the end of the day you may be feeling low and depressed, go into your room for a short while to meditate on heaven, and come out to face a sinful world with a new resolve to battle against all the injustices in our society.

3) Temptations
Is temptation your experience? The Puritans used to speak of besetting sins. In one of his Welsh hymns William Williams, Pantycelyn, speaks of falling a hundred times into the same sin. We all have that one sin which makes us vulnerable, that weakness which the evil one attacks so frequently that our soul is both wearied and depressed. It gets us down, does it not? Then, when we already feel weak and powerless, the fiery darts of the wicked are hurled at us. Totally unexpected things suddenly waylay us and set upon us, and we feel dispirited; we have failed once again in the battle against the evil one and his wiles. The suddenness is astounding: you wake up in the morning, and before you have

decided what day of the week it is, a thought comes into your head—an unsavoury thought, a cruel thought, a proud thought, a covetous thought. And these attacks come so regularly.

There are temptations all around us in the society in which we live. A generation ago you were protected from many of them. If you lived within the orbit of the chapel and a restricted circle of acquaintances, these temptations did not come your way. But nowadays they all come into your home via the television and the daily paper. I feel sure that as believers we make every effort to fight against the temptations that bombard us from all directions, but it has to be confessed that we fail badly day after day, and we get to feel battle-weary.

Do you sometimes feel, at the end of the day, that you have spent all your energy fighting against temptation; that you are so drained that you cannot face your proper work? Do you feel so downcast because of your constant failure that you are driven to brood miserably in a corner?

It is, of course, the devil who is behind it all, as Paul tells us in his letter to the Ephesians: 'For we do not wrestle against flesh and blood, but against principalities, against powers, against the rulers of the darkness of this age, against spiritual hosts of wickedness in the heavenly places' (Ephesians 6:12). That is the battle we fight, a battle against the evil one himself and his minions.

What remedy is there when all is dark and we are huddled in our corner, not knowing where to turn? Have you tried meditating on heaven? Listen once more to the book of Revelation: 'He laid hold of the dragon, that serpent of old, who is the Devil and Satan, and bound him for a thousand years; and he cast him into the bottomless pit, and shut him up, and set a seal on him . . .' (20:2-3). And again in the same chapter we are told: 'And the devil, who deceived them, was cast into the lake of fire and brimstone where the beast and the false prophet are. And they will be tormented day and night for ever and ever' (verse 10). Think of heaven! You will wake up one morning with no unsavoury thoughts, no enmity—heaven indeed! The devil will be barred entry, all his dominions and principalities will be powerless, the bows that gave flight to his fiery darts will be useless. We shall be free of him for ever. Small wonder the hymnist rejoices at the prospect!

> *Sin, my worst enemy before,*
> *Shall vex my eyes and ears no more;*
> *My inward foes shall all be slain,*
> *Nor Satan break my peace again.*
>
> Isaac Watts

No sin! If, then, you feel that the furnaces are getting too hot, retire to your room and meditate on heaven. And come out enabled to withstand in the evil day, knowing that our light affliction in this world is but for a moment, and that before us is a day when we shall be free from all temptations.

4) Persecution

We need to be rather reticent in speaking of persecution, knowing as we do that there are Christians in this world who know what it means to be *really* persecuted. Yet we sometimes need to deal with the kind of persecution that comes our way. Perhaps some of you are constantly persecuted in the workplace: colleagues are always provoking you and making fun of your faith; you are subjected to frequent 'digs', snide remarks, subtle leg-pulling; or you are being ignored or sent to Coventry—and it is all sapping your energy. Dealing with this kind of sly behaviour from someone who would never strike you or stab you with a knife is worrying; it disturbs the peace of the soul and preys on the mind.

What comfort is there for us in heaven? Listen once more to the book of Revelation:

Then one of the elders answered, saying to me, 'Who are these arrayed in white robes, and where did they come from?' And I said to him, 'Sir, you know.' So he said to me, 'These are the ones who came out of the great tribulation, and washed their robes and made them white in the blood of the Lamb. Therefore they are before the throne of God, and serve him day and night in his temple. And he who sits on the throne will dwell among them' (7:13-15).

I have promised not to complicate matters by dealing with the theology of these things, but here we have the term 'great tribulation'. As you know, there are some who maintain that it refers to a great persecution of the saints shortly before the second coming; others believe it refers to the persecution of the saints down the ages, that is, during the period between the first coming of our Lord and his second coming. But whichever way you interpret the term, it obviously refers to a persecution of the saints.

It is to these words, however, that I wish to draw your attention: 'these are the ones who *came out* of the great tribulation'. Whatever the nature or the time of the persecution, those who are in heaven have come out of it! You will not be getting up in the morning worrying about whether your colleagues are going to make fun of you; you will be out of the 'great tribulation' for ever!

It is interesting to note what consolation Jesus offers his disciples when, in the Sermon on the Mount, he refers to the persecution that lies ahead. 'Blessed are those who are persecuted for righteousness' sake, for theirs is the kingdom of heaven.' He does not say that that they shall be comforted, or that they shall obtain mercy, but assures them that the kingdom of heaven is already theirs. That is their salvation, that is their consolation in the midst of suffering.

And then he goes on to say: 'Blessed are you when they revile and persecute you, and say all kinds of evil against you falsely for my sake. Rejoice and be exceedingly glad, for great is your reward in heaven' (Matthew 5:11-12).

So our Lord's prescribed remedy when we are disheartened by persecution is to think of the place that awaits us—to meditate on heaven. Who knows that there might not be more severe persecution awaiting evangelical Christians in the coming years? Perhaps many of us will be called to suffer for Christ's sake. What better thing can we do than retire to meditate on heaven, in order to come out revitalised, aware of the fact that we shall not have to contend against our enemies for ever? There is a place of eternal rest for the saints.

5) Death

Here is another factor that oppresses us. Secular society believes that all life is the product of evolution, and that all living creatures, humans and animals, die and cease to exist. Men die, they are buried, and that is the end. Indeed, one of our Welsh-language poets of the twentieth century expressed it thus:

> *When all our foolish flustering is o'er,*
> *Into vast silence shall we slip once more.*
>
> (tr.)

There are two ways in which death affects us. First, there is the death of someone near and dear; the sudden, unexpected, bitter bereavement perhaps, with the mourning, sadness and pain that follow. And then there is our own death. Even good Christians can be afraid of 'the last enemy', although some may be too ashamed to confess their fear. I remember a lady asking me whether it was wrong to be a little afraid of dying. 'I would never tell them in chapel,' she said, 'in case they doubted my faith.' But there is nothing wrong with being afraid. There is an awesomeness about death.

31

This is how the Welsh hymnist puts it:

> Deep Jordan's banks I tread
> And, trembling, waver;
> I long to cross, but dread
> The stormy river.
> O would 'twere given that I
> Might shun these swellings high,
> And o'er the flood might fly,
> To rest for ever!
>
> The stream in might along
> Its waters urges,
> And many are the strong
> The wave submerges.
> I fear the land of light
> Will never greet my sight,
> And I shall sink tonight
> Beneath these surges.

(tr.)

It is not unusual for believers to have problems with dying. The death of dear ones does cause sadness and pain, and the inevitability of the fact that there will come a time when each of us will have to bid farewell to this earth creates fear and doubt.

How are we to deal with this last enemy? Have you tried meditating on heaven? What is true about that place? What did the apostle John see, according to Revelation 21:2-4?

Then I saw the holy city, new Jerusalem, coming down out of heaven from God, prepared as a bride adorned for her husband. And I heard a loud voice from heaven saying, 'Behold, the tabernacle of God is with men, and he will dwell with them, and they shall be his people, and God himself will be

32

with them, and be their God. And God will wipe away every tear from their eyes; there shall be no more death, nor sorrow, nor crying.'

This is paradise: knowing that a dear one will not be snatched away; that there is no enemy to face; there shall be no more death. 'And death shall have no dominion.'

What lies ahead of us? It will not be a matter of slipping back into the vast silence whence we came, but, as another Welsh poet has put it:

> Into the harbour, where no storm
> My bark can overwhelm,
> I'll sail triumphantly one day:
> My Father's at the helm.

The third stanza of the hymn quoted above puts it thus:

> But who are these I see
> In crowds appearing?
> Old friends, from peril free,
> My spirit cheering.
> I'll linger here no more,
> But trust to God that bore
> Them safe to yonder shore,
> No danger fearing.
>
> (tr.)

Difficult providences, the presence of sin, temptations, persecution and death—those are the five things that cause us to become low in spirit. But they all spring from a common source, the devil. Who was responsible for the coming of sin into the world? Why did the earth have to be cursed? Who is the perpetrator of every persecution? The evil one. Why is death inevitable? It is the wages of sin, our inheritance through Adam. Do you despise the devil? Do you hate sin, the curse upon the earth, all the suffering that plagues the human race because of his malice and cunning? We must deal with him now; we must look to something to set us firmly on our feet. What better than to look to the glory that is to come, so that we can return to the world of sin and curse, of persecution and temptation, of wickedness and death, with a new resolve to face them and battle against them patiently, doing as much as we possibly can to alleviate the pain and sadness around us, in the sure hope that soon we shall be freed from them all?

My soul, thy face no longer hide,
The way to heaven is open wide;
Our enemies are now in chains,
Satan is vanquished: Jesus reigns!

(tr.)

3
Pleasures
here and beyond

As we have pointed out, life has its difficult experiences. But it also has its pleasurable ones, and we are now going to approach heaven from another angle: that of enjoying life and the pleasures of this world. There are several ways of describing this modern age in which we live, and one of the words that surfaces continually is 'hedonistic'. We belong to an age which has the pursuit of pleasure at the top of its agenda. Nowadays the highest salaries are those offered by the entertainment business, one of the chief industries of modern Britain. The big earners of our day are the pop singers, the actors, the sports stars. Ours is the age of the television, the video and the exotic holidays. People now look for all kinds of sensuous and pleasurable experiences. And as we know, many of those who experiment and who search for these experiences ultimately find themselves enticed into the world of drugs. We live in a sensuous, relaxed age, where everything has to be fun and excitement.

And we must expect the situation to get worse. People's working week is continually getting shorter; there is more leisure time. The present Government has seen fit to appoint a minister to be responsible for leisure pursuits; local authorities have the onerous task of providing and financing well-equipped leisure centres, and as the years progress the demand will become ever greater.

The experts who analyse these trends realise how dangerous it is for a society to become pleasure-centred. When that happens, they contend, creative energy is undermined and people become spineless; they are no longer moved by that indomitable urge to accomplish things. This is how, some years ago, *Time* magazine described the situation in America:

> The deepest American dilemma regarding excellence arises from the nation's success; the United States has been an astonishing phenomenon, excellent among the nations of the world, but as the prophet Amos said: 'Woe to them who are at ease in Zion'. It is possible to have repose or to have excellence. Success has cost Americans something of their energetic desire.

Do you see what happens? Success comes; people begin to relax and enjoy the pleasure of that success, and by so doing they lose their creative energy and the desire for distinction evaporates.

This is how Tennessee Williams succinctly phrased it: 'One does not easily escape from the seduction of an effete way of life; with conflict removed man is a sword cutting daisies.' Now that the old enemy, Communism, has largely disappeared, America seems not to know how to manage its affairs. The problem of pleasure and ease raises its head, especially since there is so much chasing after sexual satisfaction. 'The regime that permits chronically excessive, illicit and disorderly sex activities contributes to the decline of cultural activity.' When the pursuit of pleasure moves to the sexual realm, it is especially harmful to society and completely undermines its creative activity.

Sadly, it has to be said that the Western society in which we as Christians live is just such a society. This means that, in future years, we shall have to live amongst people who devote themselves to pursuing pleasure. The question is, How are we to deal with that? What will be our response? Already we are seeing the effect of this influence, even in the evangelical world. For

36

instance, a recent poster announcing the visit of a certain preacher urged people to come and listen to his 'relaxing ministry'; and a church service I heard announced was described as a 'fun time'. Everything must be pleasurable; it seems not to matter whether the worship is in spirit and in truth.

As children of our time, it is so easy for us as evangelical Christians to be caught up in this relentless pursuit of pleasure, and to find ourselves sucked into the maelstrom of seeking the next 'fun' experience. No longer are we satisfied with what we already have. Granted, we may wish to keep within the guidelines of God's Word—its moral standards, for instance; but we can become exhausted in rushing after legitimate pleasures such as hobbies, sports, physical fitness, concerts, *eisteddfodau*, exotic holidays, television programmes, videos. Soon we shall find that our creative energy and enthusiasm are being drained. Are you a Sunday school teacher? Have you ever rushed your preparation for the coming lesson in order to see a programme on TV or go to a play? Yes, the pursuit of pleasure affects the work of the Christian.

How, then, are we to deal with this problem? Are we to deny ourselves the pleasures of this world, and live up to our reputation of being long-faced killjoys? Should we enjoy life, especially when there is so much suffering around us and so many disasters worldwide? Do we sometimes feel guilty that we are enjoying life when we see particularly distressing pictures on our television screens? How are we to reconcile our pleasures with the problems and the need around us, and how are we to view everything within a life of Christian service?

There is only one answer. Just as we dealt with suffering and life's problems in the light of heaven, so must we deal with the question of pleasure. By doing so we shall find ourselves freed from the desiring and the seeking that characterise the worldly man, who, after all, has no future pleasures to look forward to. As believers, we need to remind ourselves that this world's pleasures are transient—they fade away; but the pleasures that await us in heaven are not only greater, but everlasting.

A glimpse of paradise
When dealing with the pain and affliction of this world, we saw how important it is to meditate on the things that are *not* in heaven. But in dealing with the problem of hankering and seeking after pleasure, we will derive more comfort from meditating on the things that *are* there—the pleasure that lies in store for God's people.

The saints
Heaven will be full of saints—but I hasten to add, in case there is someone who finds the company of certain individuals trying, they will be *sanctified* saints. Do we not sometimes wonder why as believers we can be so awkward? We fall out and disagree; we make mountains out of molehills. It all stems from the curse, sin, this carnal body. The evil one muddies the waters and stirs up hatred and envy. He plays on our pride, our self-importance, our oversensitivity or our lack of sensitivity. These things can mar our relationship with our fellow Christians to such an extent that their company here on earth is far from heavenly.

But in heaven the old body will have been made new, and the devil will not be there to plague our minds with suggestive, malicious thoughts. We shall certainly be worth knowing there! The most awkward saint you have ever met, the meekest, the quietest, the one who never ventured out of his corner—whoever it be, in paradise it will be a privilege to be in their company!

Let us not, however, paint too dark a picture of saints here below. There have been times when we have all said that fellowship has been sweet, and when we have said 'This is good.' We agree with the Welsh hymnist:

Sweet the company of brothers
  Fellow pilgrims on the way;
Not one tongue content to flatter,
  Nor one bosom to betray:
Heaven's dew upon their discourse,
  Hope eternal 'neath their breast,
Longing for their home in glory,
  That abode of perfect rest.

(tr.)

And that is what heaven is—the home of the saints. Meditate occasionally on the everlasting pleasure of the company of transformed saints in that heavenly home.

What is more, heaven will be *full* of saints. You remember that verse in Revelation: 'After these things I looked, and behold, a great multitude, which no one could number, of all nations, tribes, peoples, and tongues, standing before the throne and before the Lamb, clothed with white robes, with palm branches in their hands' (7:9). What a consolation that is for those who speak minority languages! Those of us who worship in Welsh frequently suffer from the small congregation syndrome. While we claim the promise 'where two or three are gathered in my name, there I am in the midst', we secretly long for the five or six, the dozens, the hundreds. Would there not be more power in the worship, more arms to uphold the preacher, more concerted longing, a greater sense of communion around the Lord's table? Well, in heaven there will be no empty seats; heaven will be full of people of every tribe, nation and language, and we shall have the pleasure of worshipping with a countless throng of brothers and sisters.

God himself
God himself is in heaven. No one has ever seen God, but in heaven we shall see him face to face. 'And I heard a loud voice

from heaven saying, "Behold, the tabernacle of God is with men, and he will dwell with them, and they shall be his people, and God himself will be with them and be their God"' (Revelation 21:3). When, in this world, we are privileged with an occasional glimpse of his glory, there is always a measure of awe because we are still in this mortal body. You remember Isaiah's reaction on seeing the glory of God in the temple. Although it was a wonderful and joyful experience, there was a measure of fear and terror, and he wished he could hide himself. When we come face to face with God in heaven the wonder and joy will still be there, but the fear will have gone. The corruption which is a feature of our mortal make-up will no longer exist; we shall appear before God clothed in incorruptible, immortal bodies. And God—yes, God himself! —will wipe the tears from our eyes.

Jesus Christ

The Lord Jesus Christ will be in heaven. I feel sure that God will be well pleased if we spend more time dealing with this point. This is how John tells us of the presence of the Lord Jesus Christ in heaven: 'And I looked, and behold, in the midst of the throne and of the four living creatures, and in the midst of the elders, stood a Lamb as though it had been slain' (Revelation 5:6).

Notice what John sees: not Christ the Messiah, not the Prince of princes and King of kings, but 'a Lamb as though it had been slain'. Twenty-eight times does the apostle see the second person of the Trinity, the Son of God, seated upon his throne, and with very few exceptions the title given him is 'the Lamb'. We need not wonder at this. John is fully aware that the presence of the saints in heaven is totally dependent on the sacrifice made on their behalf—on the Son, 'the Lamb', having been slain.

To appreciate the significance of the term 'Lamb' we have to turn back to the Old Testament. You remember how God initiated a system of sacrifices whereby the Israelites might have

40

forgiveness of their sins. Central to that system was the lamb without blemish, the perfect lamb. It is difficult for us to imagine how things were under the old dispensation. Countless animals were sacrificed daily, monthly, annually; the temple was always awash with blood. Not only was it a costly business (one can imagine the stereotypical Jew loath to part with his tithe, let alone the best of his flock!), but it would appear wasteful. But God was trying to press home upon his people the exceeding sinfulness of sin and the exceeding costliness of forgiveness. That was the purpose behind it. It was not that God desired the slaughter of these innocent animals, but that he would have the nation realise the gravity of sin, the inevitability of punishment, and the cost of propitiation.

But we have to go even further back than the sacrificial system—back to the end of Israel's captivity in Egypt and the institution of the Passover. After Pharoah had nine times refused to let the people go, God warned him that he would kill every male first-born of man and animal throughout his kingdom. To escape the vengeance of the angel of death the Jews were told to slaughter a lamb, smear the upper post and side posts of the door with its blood, and remain inside the house. The sign of the blood would ensure their safety from the angel's destruction, and henceforth the Paschal lamb would remind them of that great deliverance. It also serves to remind us that only shed blood can turn away the wrath of a righteous God.

Now there are dramatic moments in the history of man, are there not?—moments when individuals make certain pronouncements that affect the future of the world. Such was the moment when Archimedes shouted 'Eureka', having discovered his famous principle. Such was the moment when, while the whole world held its breath, the first American astronaut to set foot on the moon said the unforgettable words, 'One small step for man; one giant step for mankind.'

But if you were to ask me who made the most astounding, the most wonderful, the most uplifting pronouncement ever made, I would take you back two millennia to the banks of the Jordan, where a rough-looking John the Baptist was baptising repentant sinners. Seeing his cousin (six months younger than he) approaching, he loudly proclaimed: 'Behold! The Lamb of God who takes away the sin of the world!' (John 1:29). He had the unique privilege of telling the people that the One who was the substance of all the sacrifices of the past had come among them; that the pattern of the Paschal Lamb was going to be fulfilled before their eyes.

It was a great moment in the history of mankind. God's purpose from eternity was to be accomplished in the incarnate Son. As the Lamb of God, he would shed his blood so that sinners might be set free. No wonder the other John saw none but the Lamb having been slain, the One who had come to secure our release from the clutches of sin and death.

From the fifth chapter of Revelation we get the clear impression that everyone in heaven finds pleasure in praising the Lamb. There are numerous choirs.

> The four living creatures and the twenty-four elders fell down before the Lamb, each having a harp, and golden bowls full of incense, which are the prayers of the saints. And they sang a new song, saying, 'You are worthy to take the scroll, and to open its seals; for you were slain, and have redeemed us to God by your blood out of every tribe and tongue and people and nation, and have made us kings and priests to our God; and we shall reign on the earth.'

Small wonder that they sing! They realise what they have been rescued from, and the privileged position they now enjoy.

But there is a second choir:

Then I looked, and I heard the voice of many angels around the throne, the living creatures, and the elders; and the number of them was ten thousand times ten thousand, and thousands of thousands, saying with a loud voice, 'Worthy is the Lamb who was slain to receive power and riches and wisdom, and strength and honour and glory and blessing!'

And there is yet a third choir:

And every creature which is in heaven and on the earth and under the earth and such as are in the sea, and all that are in them, heard I saying: 'Blessing and honour and glory and power be to him who sits on the throne, and to the Lamb, for ever and ever.' Then the four living creatures said, 'Amen!' And the twenty-four elders fell down and worshipped him who lives for ever and ever.

To be in heaven and among those choristers is the ultimate pleasure for a mere mortal. And to be there in the presence of the Lamb!

Our attitude to life's pleasures
What then of the pleasures of this world? This is what the book of Ecclesiastes has to say:

Nothing is better for a man than that he should eat and drink, and that his soul should enjoy good in his labour. This also, I saw, was from the hand of God. For who can eat, or who can have enjoyment, more than I? For God gives wisdom and knowledge and joy to a man . . . (2:24-26).

I know that . . . every man should eat and drink and enjoy the good of all his labour—it is the gift of God (3:12,13).

As for every man to whom God has given riches and wealth, and given him power to eat of it, to receive his heritage and rejoice in his labour—this is the gift of God (5:19).

So I commended enjoyment, because a man has nothing better under the sun than to eat, drink, and be merry; for this will remain with him in his labour for the days of his life which God gives him under the sun (8:15).

Truly the light is sweet, and it is pleasant for the eyes to behold the sun (11:7).

We are to enjoy all the blessings of this life bestowed upon us by God, but within the moral parameters set down by him. The creation, the good gifts of his providence, marital relationship, children, art and culture, music and literature—all are there for us to enjoy. God's gifts to humanity are for his people too; we insult him if, amidst all his blessings, we are niggardly and sour-faced. We need to enjoy his gifts as they come our way, thanking him for them.

The fact that heaven has greater pleasures in store for us should set us free from hankering after forbidden pleasures and rushing after the ephemeral things of this world. So, when tempted by the devil to satisfy our baser desires, we can withdraw for a while to meditate on heaven and see things in their right perspective, and come out feeling relaxed and content. The energy we would have wasted chasing hither and thither will be available to serve God and promote his kingdom.

The truth is this. As believers we have the best of both worlds: we can enjoy our present God-given pleasures in the certain knowledge that the best pleasures are yet to come. How should that affect us? It should teach us to enjoy our life here below, keeping our eyes steadfastly on the pleasures awaiting us. We should then find that a new enthusiasm has been released—a burning desire to serve our Lord and Master.

Then we discover something else. The greatest satisfaction in this world is that derived from work finished, service completed, duty done. The greatest pleasure is derived not from what society has to offer but from doing God's will. The greatest satisfaction, the greatest pleasure that we can have in this world, is in his service.

> *In Thy work I find my life-spring,*
> *In Thy work I find my peace.*
>
> (tr.)

Heaven, then, is a place full of sanctified saints, the Father attending to each one personally, the Lamb who was slain being the focus of their praise.

4
Work and rest

The amount of work that faces us as Christians in our day and age is staggering. Cast your mind back to the book of Genesis. There man was told to cultivate the earth and make it fruitful. The toil involved in that alone would appear to be sufficient to occupy the saints! But today, because of our mismanagement of God's creation, we have the added problem of pollution to contend with. Small wonder the ecological sciences are crying out for committed, dedicated workers! But we must bear in mind that cultivating the earth involves more than agriculture and horticulture. It encompasses culture of all kinds—literature, music, art—and we are to be equally involved in cultivating any skills we may have in that direction.

In Genesis we also find God instituting the family, and that reminds us of another responsibility we have to shoulder. We are to be the husbands and wives, the parents and children that God expects us to be. And that is no mean achievement!

The pattern of the working week is also set: a reminder that we are not only to employ ourselves usefully, but we are to be good, diligent, honest workers wherever we might find ourselves. Our aim in the workplace must be to please God rather than man.

Moving on to the New Testament, we are reminded that we are to be the salt of the earth: that is, that influence for good which will prevent the spread of sin's pollution. When we look at our society we realise the enormity of the task. Nonetheless we are told to withstand evil. And this entails tackling the moral and social questions that are continually brought to our notice.

As believers, the New Testament also commands us to do good works—acts of love and mercy towards those in society who are facing problems of all kinds—'that they may see your good works and glorify your Father in heaven'. And we are not to grow weary in the doing!

Then there is our responsibility to the local church. We are to be prepared to participate fully in the life of the church. Not content with being mere passengers, we are to contribute to the corporate life of the church. There is no shortage of work for church members: we need preachers and ministers, secretaries and treasurers, Sunday school teachers, visitors of the sick and the housebound, prayer warriors and givers. There is work to be done.

Personal devotions, of course, must not be neglected. We need to set aside time to read the Word and pray, and also, in view of what has already been said about meditating on heaven, to digest what we have heard and read.

Added to all this, or basic to it, is the great commission: 'Go into all the world and preach the gospel to every creature.' Our primary task as Christians is to fill heaven. The epitaph on Daniel Rowland's memorial reminds us how empty the corners of heaven would be were it not for 'Zion' (the church) nurturing saints on earth. The seraph-preacher of Llangeitho, and others similarly anointed by the Spirit of God, certainly helped to fill them in their day. Times have changed, and true religion is at a low ebb here in Wales. Our task is to call this nation of ours back to God and to Christ, so that the corners of heaven will begin to fill once more. And there are still people throughout the world who continue to wait for the good news so that they also will find a place in heaven. As we contemplate the pleasures that await us, do we not feel obligated to see that they hear the gospel? Yes, there is much work to be done.

We shall have rest in heaven
We are all agreed that our land is in dire need of totally committed

Christian workers (not necessarily full-time workers), who will labour steadfastly and untiringly in the service of the Lord Jesus Christ. This final reason why we should meditate on heaven should further motivate believers to set to work with new vigour.

Let me take you back to my college days in Aberystwyth. You began revising for examinations in a small way in January, but as the day of reckoning drew nearer the pace quickened, until, during the last few weeks, you were working from dawn till dusk trying to 'cram' as many facts and figures as possible. Three more weeks to go and, imagining that no one on earth knows more than you do, you suddenly feel overcome with fatigue and are ready to throw in the towel. To add to your distress, the sun is shining, the sea is an inviting blue, and visitors from the Midlands are strolling noisily along the prom! And to cap it all, some of your fellow students either have no exams or have finished their exams.

At such a time, what gives you the incentive to persevere? What enables you to say to yourself, 'In three weeks' time it will all be over'? Well, it is the 'heaven' ahead—four long, sunny, carefree months at home in Ammanford! The very thought drives you back to your studies, not with enthusiasm perhaps, but with an iron determination to see the task through.

Do you sometimes feel like giving up? Then you must step aside and meditate on that place where there will be rest after life's sweat and toil. Dealing with the verse 'In my Father's house are many mansions . . .' (John 14:2), one commentator interprets the Greek word translated 'mansions' as 'resting places'. Jesus Christ is here saying that he is going to prepare many places for weary saints to rest.

Hebrews 4:9-11 is more explicit: 'There remains therefore a rest for the people of God. For he who has entered his rest has himself also ceased from his works as God did from his. Let us therefore be diligent to enter that rest . . .' The fact that there is rest after all the work should encourage us to persevere. Now is not the time to down tools; now is not the time to rest. When all the work is brought to an end, to the glory of God, then will be the time to rest.

Have you ever had difficulty trying to rest? Although conscious that you need a good night's sleep after a particularly busy and tiring day, you go to bed and you just cannot doze off—all kinds of things dart through your mind. Perhaps you live on your own, and you spend the night listening for any suspicious noise in the house; and you get up in the morning feeling more tired than you did before going to bed. In order to have proper rest one must be free from tensions, and there must be a feeling of security. When, at the end of a trying day spent dealing with some family problem, someone says, 'Don't worry, I'll see to that', you go to bed relaxed, secure in the knowledge that the other person has shouldered the responsibility. The small child who is scared of intruders entering the house will sleep like a log when told by his father, 'Leave that to Dad. He'll take care of things.'

Heaven will be completely free of the cares and tensions that now trouble you; nor will there be thieves breaking in and stealing. God will say, 'Rest. *I* am here; *I* will see to everything', and we shall have true rest for the very first time. And it will bear no comparison with that 'good night's sleep' we so value here below. In heaven, we shall feel security wrapped around us like a blanket.

But I hasten to add that there will be no laziness in heaven. Indeed, if we were idle for eternity, heaven would be a very uninteresting place! Do you remember how, during exams, I used to look forward to that long, sun-drenched holiday, doing absolutely no academic work? Oftener than not on that holiday I would find myself doing exactly what I had done before the exams—reading books for hours. The activity was the same, but there was a difference: one was work, the other pleasure; one was *before* the day of reckoning, the other when it was past!

In heaven, life's labour will be over. Beyond the Day of Judgement, work will be synonymous with pleasure. Revelation 7:15 tells us what we shall be doing: serving God 'day and night in his temple'; praising the Lamb who secured for us the 'many mansions'. Serving God here on earth can sometimes be an effort: there are troubles, and there is weariness. But in heaven it will be effortless, free of toil and stress. The seats will not be hard, nor the time 'endless'; the sermon will not be too long, nor the service 'boring'! Work and rest will have become one.

Have you ever felt like giving up? Have you ever said, 'I can't be a Sunday school teacher! I've done enough; it's time I had some rest'? Have you felt that the effort of serving the Lord is 'too much'? The best antidote to Satan's suggestions is a period of meditation on heaven. Having realised that an eternity of perfect rest lies before you, you will come out of your room feeling refreshed, and as determined to persevere as I was during exam times long ago.

Our sphere of work

Seeing that there is so much work to be done, some of us might be tempted to try doing it all ourselves. But we cannot possibly deal with every social problem; we cannot share the gospel with every single person in the area; we cannot read every book, pray every prayer. Therefore the question that each one of us has to settle is this. What is my appointed task in my local area, and in the work in general in our land? Unless we know how we can best contribute to the Lord's work we might be wasting our time and energy doing either what we are unsuited for or things that are of little value.

First of all, what is your special *interest*? We are all different; we have different interests. Some of us may be interested in the geography, history and culture of a specific country; some may be concerned about social issues; some are drawn to particular people

50

within a certain group. I hardly think that God would expect us do anything that we had no interest in and found boring.

Based on that special interest, God can give us a burden. We may suddenly feel concerned about the souls of the people of a specific country; we may wish to help tackle some special social issue; we may be overwhelmed with a desire to see particular people saved. That is the first step in God's leading of his people: the special interest and burden he gives them.

Secondly, what *talent* have you? How are you gifted? All God's people have been given gifts—natural gifts and spiritual gifts, public gifts and private gifts—and we have to discover what they are, so that we may use them in association with the burden we have been given. But, human nature being what it is, we can easily deceive ourselves regarding our gifts. We may feel that we can undertake a task which in fact is well beyond our ability. That is why it is wise to consult a friend or an older Christian; they will know both our strengths and our weaknesses. And we must accept the advice given!

In summary, then, we are not to try to tackle all the work; our zeal must not lead us to attempt the impossible; our enthusiasm must be channelled to go the way the Lord leads us via a special interest and a given burden. Only then will work be accomplished to the praise and glory of his Name.

The Sabbath—a foretaste

Some of you, in your teens and twenties, may be wondering how meditating on heaven can help you, when the prospect of getting there is so far away. Has the evil one already whispered in your ear that there are many years to go before you reach the 70s or 80s, and that thinking about heaven is not much comfort? But God has foreseen the problem. Since the creation of the world he has ensured that his people are reminded of the 'eternal Sabbath', the final rest yet to come, by a divinely appointed rest day. He said, 'Six days you shall labour and do all your work, but the seventh day . . . you shall do no work'. You will be given a foretaste of heaven here on earth, to remind you of what awaits you and as an incentive to go forward in faith.

Am I right in thinking that one of the reasons why we so seldom think of heaven is the fact that our Sabbaths are no longer holy days, but so like the other six days that their special quality has been lost? If so, as you go home to meditate on heaven, go home to defend the Sabbath and to make it a foretaste of heaven.

Over the years much scorn has been poured upon the Sabbath, and it must be confessed that a certain legalism has threatened its very existence. We might well ask why our forefathers, who lived such spiritual lives, strictly forbade so many trivial things. The answer is that they were trying to make it a heavenly day. They knew that some things would not be done in heaven, and they wished to curtail the activities of the Sabbath to the minimum.

Would it not benefit us to do the same? Do we have to hear the news on the Lord's Day? Can we not wait until Monday morning to hear what the world has been up to and what the latest scandal is? Having read our weekday paper, do we have to get a Sunday paper? Rather, let us shut out the world for one day, and make the Sabbath a day of heaven. Let us each one individually consider to what degree the worldly mindset of the age has encroached upon our Sabbath. I fear that we have opened the door so wide that its heavenly quality has all but disappeared.

But not only should we strive to keep the world and its pleasures out of our Sabbaths; we should also endeavour to make them pleasurable days. We have already said that God gave us the Sabbath so that we might have a foretaste of heaven, that place where the saints, in his presence, will delight in one another's company.

In view of that, should we not seek that divine presence before attending the services? And should we not attend *both* meetings, to get better acquainted with our fellow believers? After all, is not the Sabbath a celebration of the resurrection? And what greater pleasure can there be than praising the Lamb, who was slain, but who is alive and interceding on our behalf in glory?

Then there is the pleasure of a day of rest when all the world's problems are shut out. I well remember how I used to look forward expectantly to that one day in the week when the textbooks were set aside and revision was forgotten! It was truly a foretaste of the eternal Sabbath to come.

Are you among the vast majority of people who hate Monday? Do you suffer from the 'Monday morning feeling'? If you are, there is something amiss. The Christian should be at his very best: refreshed and wide awake, ready to tackle the week's tasks with a new vigour. After all, there is another Sabbath round the corner! Small wonder the hymnist wrote, 'Make our Sabbaths days of heaven'. They are divinely ordained, so let us protect those invigorating days of rest.

There is much work to be done. The day is far gone in our land. We need to waken from our sleep, put on the armour of light, and go out to meet the foe. Are we ready to roll up our sleeves? According to the burden and the gift given us, let us show in our generation that we are not a fearful company cowering in a corner because of persecution, but people who are able to stand firm. With the sword of God's Word in our hand, his power in our heart and the glory of heaven awaiting us, no one will withstand us. There is a verse of a Welsh hymn which says:

> *In Thy work I find my life-spring,*
> *In Thy work I find my peace;*
> *In Thy work I wish to labour*
> *Till my life on earth shall cease.*
> *When, through many tribulations,*
> *I my home of rest shall see,*

> *Praising Him who died to save me*
> *Will my ceaseless service be.*
>
> (tr.)

In that day, work and rest will have become one.

Meditating on heaven will doubtless bring comfort to the Christian. But what of the unbeliever? Well, there is always the possibility that God in his mercy will remove that curtain of unbelief and give you a glimpse of glory. Do you remember the picture of Christian and Hopeful entering through the gates of heaven in *Pilgrim's Progress*? Having glimpsed the glory before him, Bunyan says, 'And after that, they shut up the Gates: which when I had seen, I wished myself among them.'

Let us not lose out on the eternal rest because of unbelief. Anyone who has not yet believed on Jesus Christ, let him make haste. Heaven is worth having. It is vital to avoid hell, yes, but heaven is worth having. And the way to get there? Believe on the Lord Jesus Christ.

> *O come, you sinners vile,*
> *The blackest earth did see,*
> *God's mercy is for you,*
> *He longs to set you free;*
> *Your frequent sins He will forget:*
> *Christ paid the ransom for your debt.*
>
> (tr.)

For whosoever repents and believes on his name there is eternal life, and heaven some day to come.